2019

Animal Coloring Book

by

Ida Jana

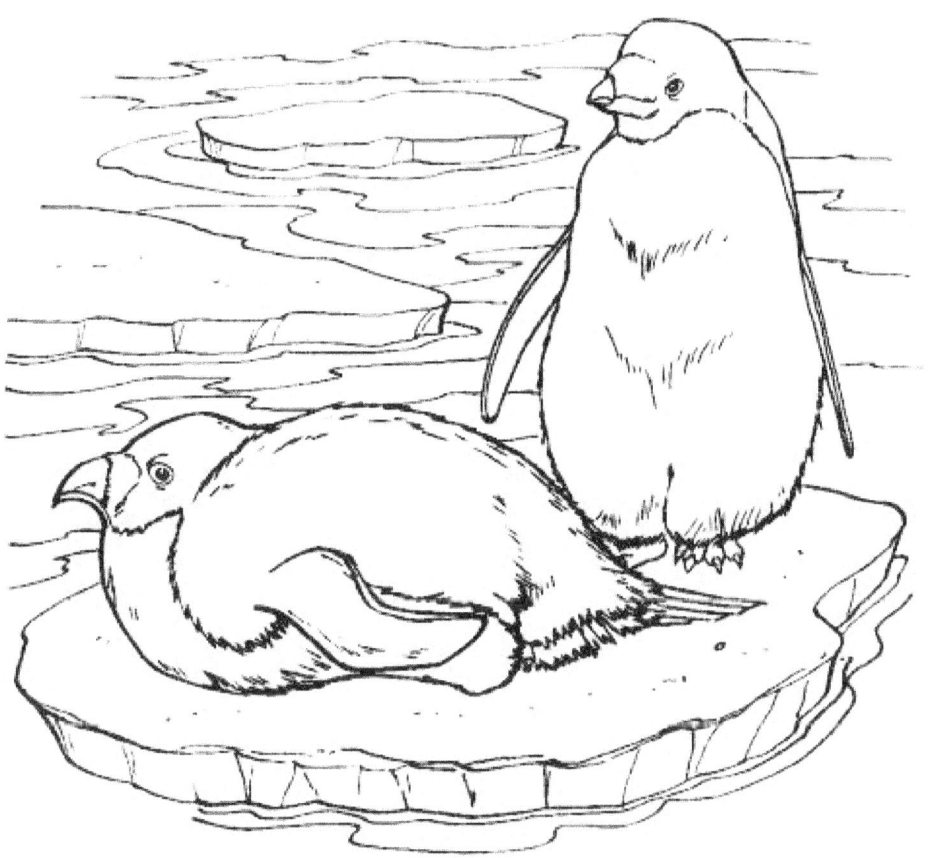

Penguins

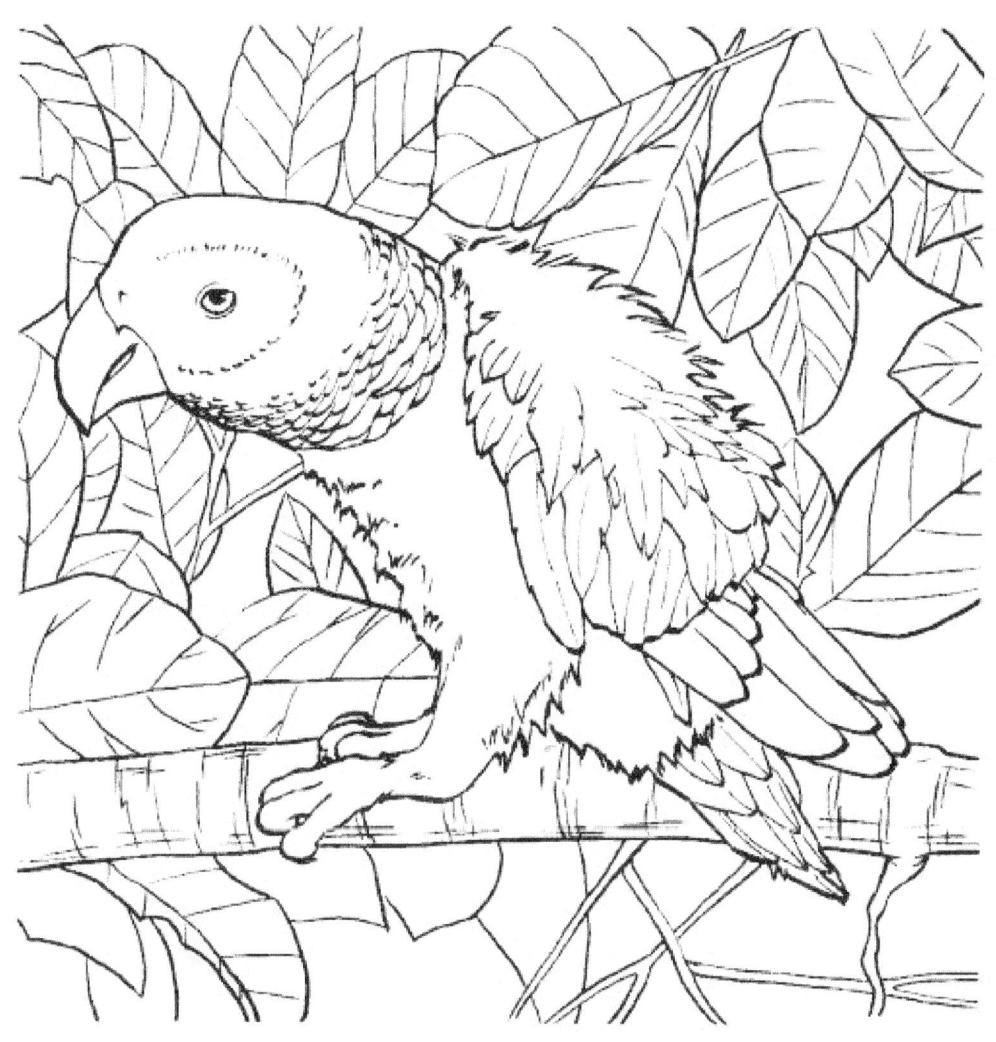

Parrots are vocal birds and
make "screaming" calls to
communicate to each other.

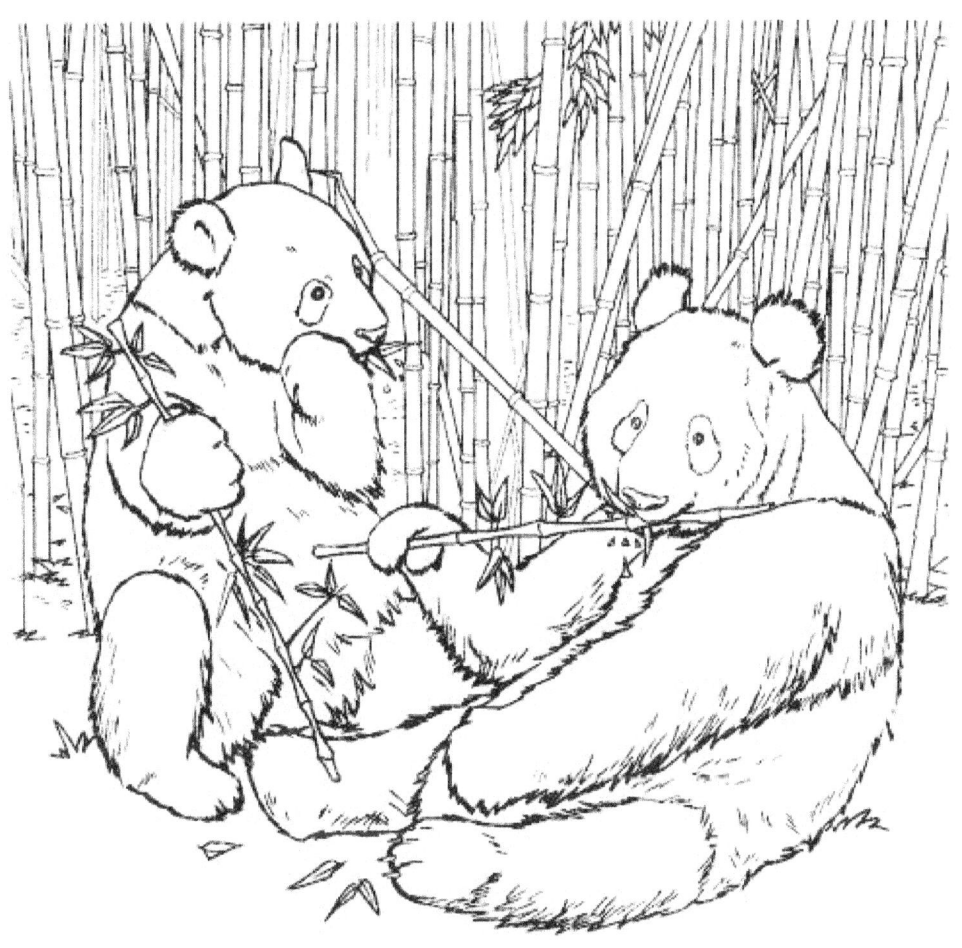

A giant panda eats up to
88 pounds of bamboo a day.

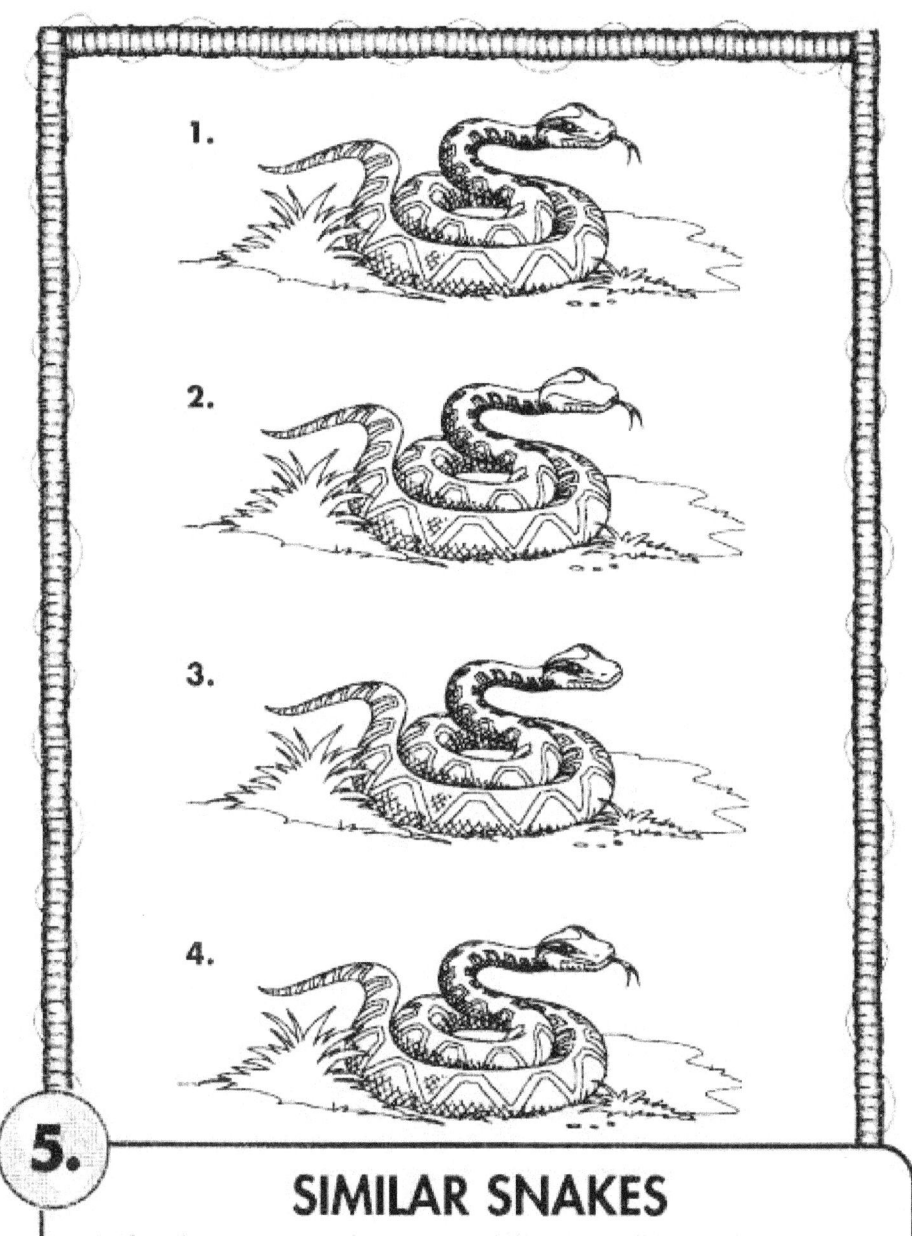

1.

2.

3.

4.

SIMILAR SNAKES

Which two snakes are identical? Circle your answer!

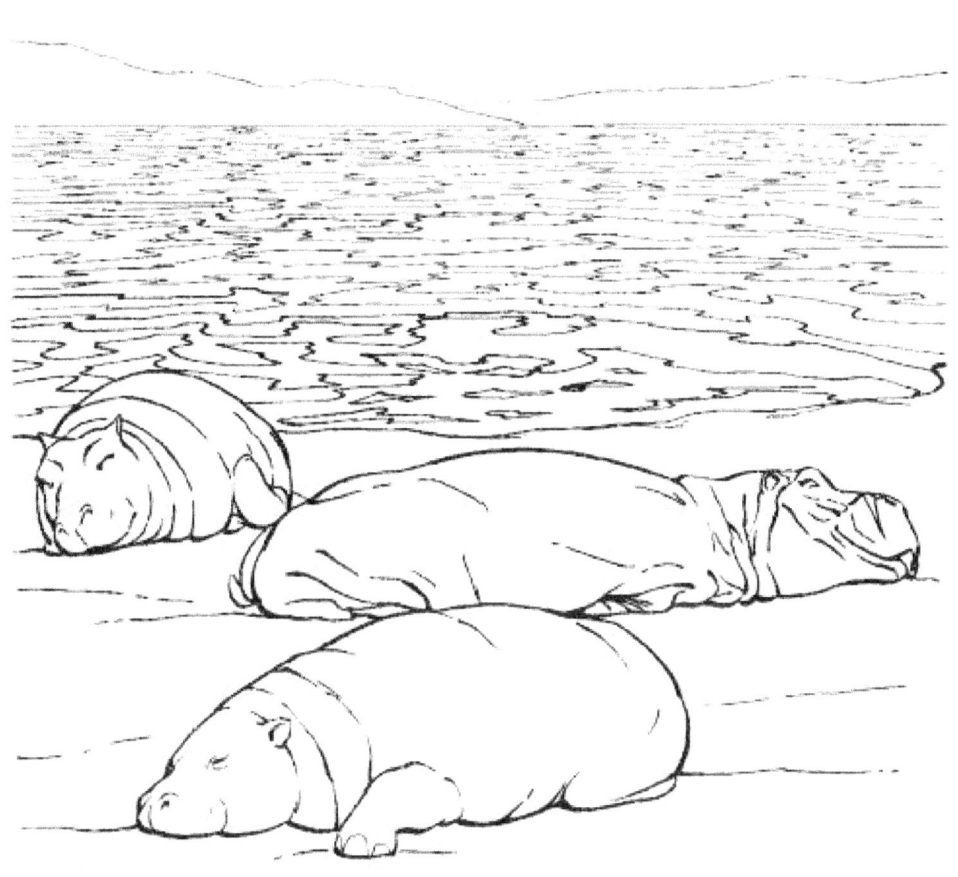

There are 2 species of
hippo, both found in Africa.

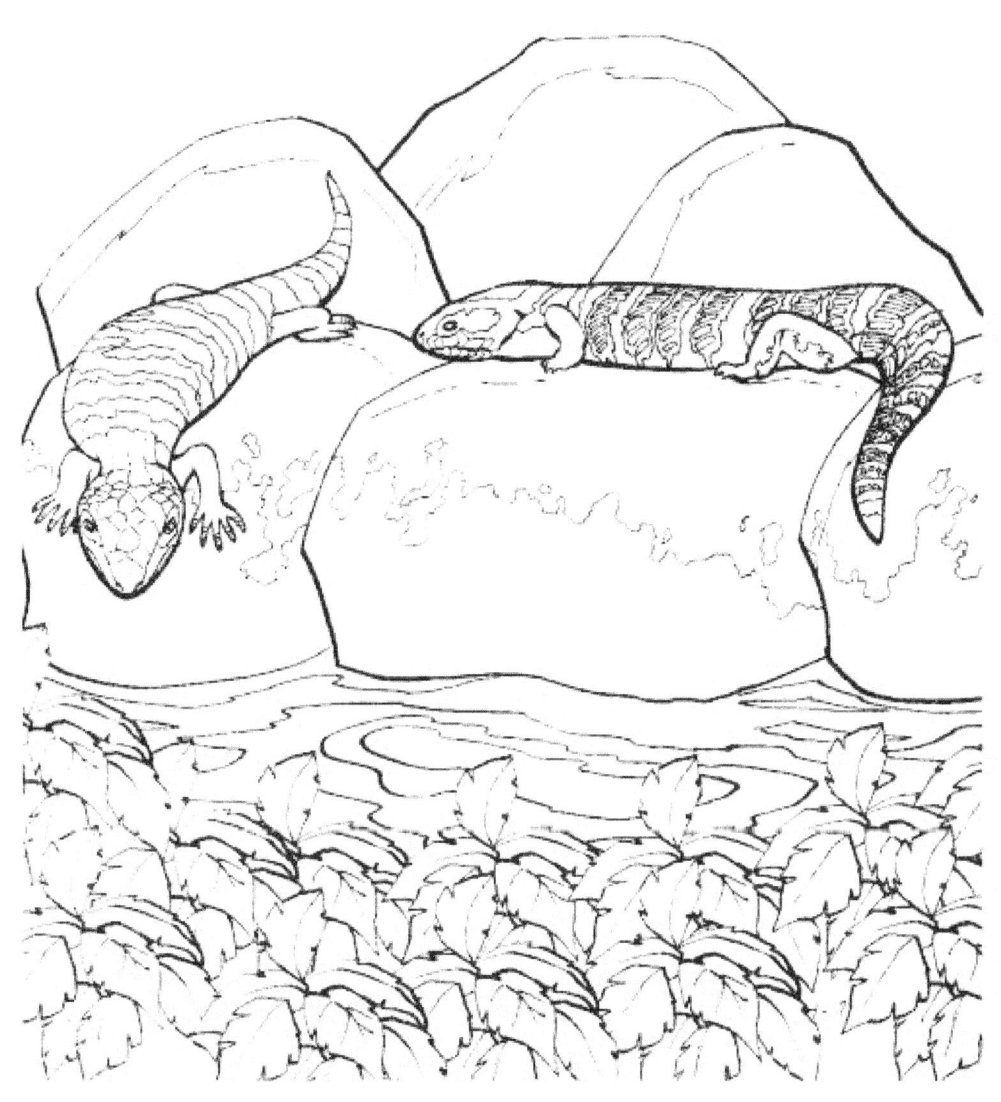

Common lizards remove the
skin on their tails to fool predators.

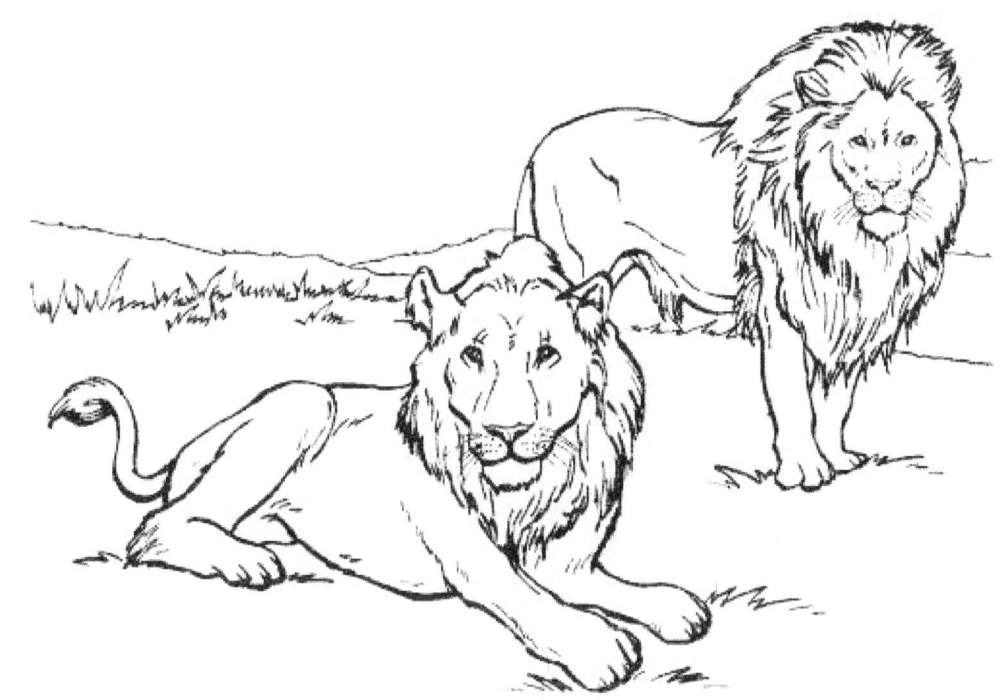

Lions

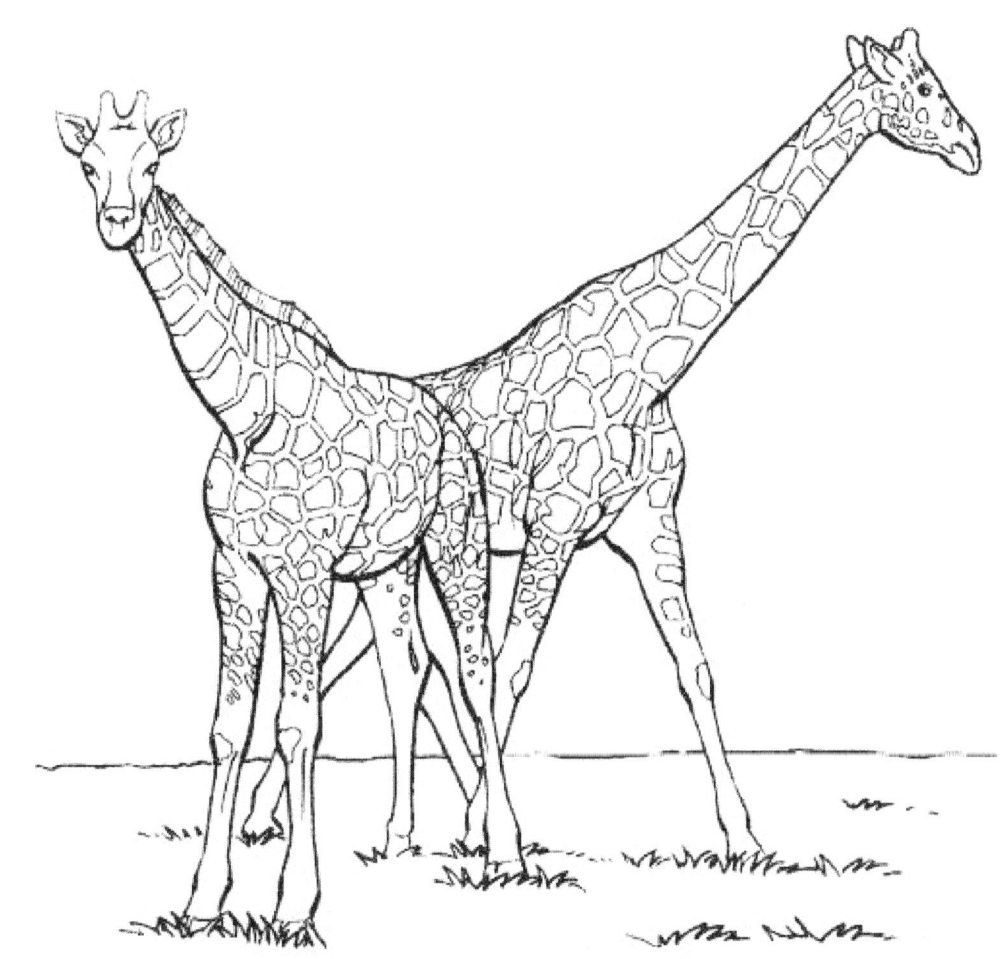

Giraffes

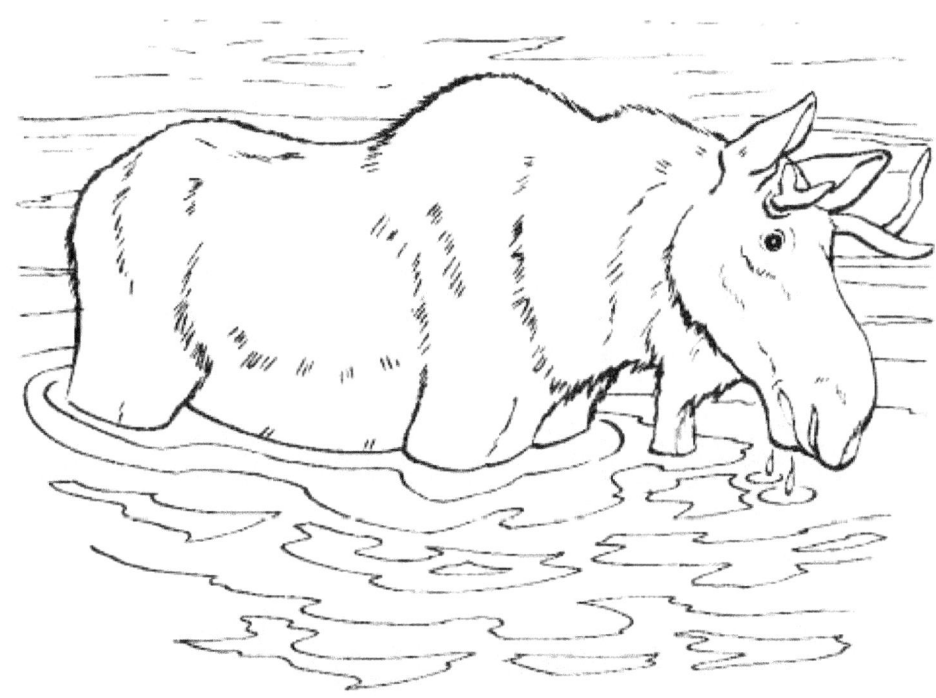

Moose

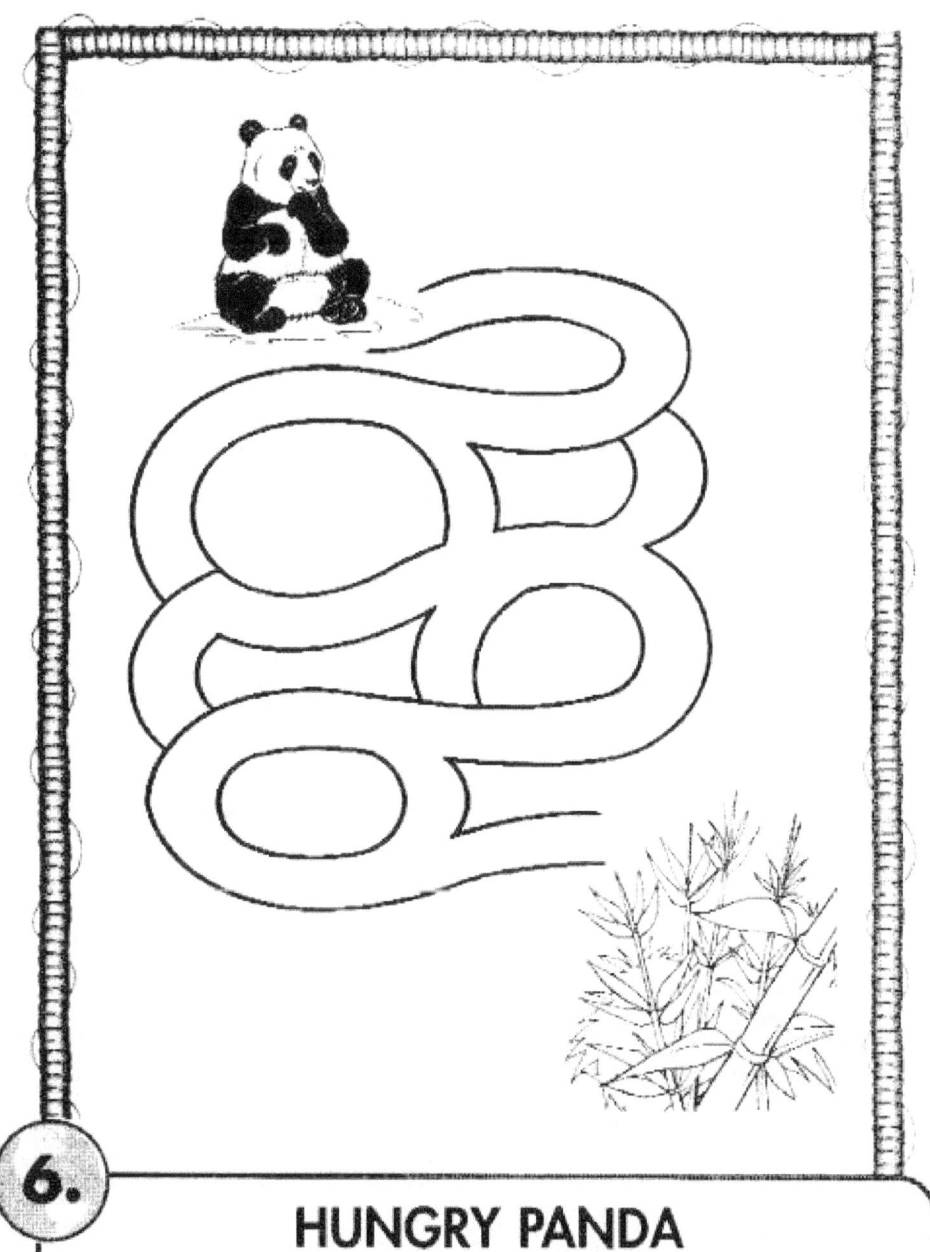

HUNGRY PANDA

Help the hungry panda bear to his bamboo
by following the path through the maze!

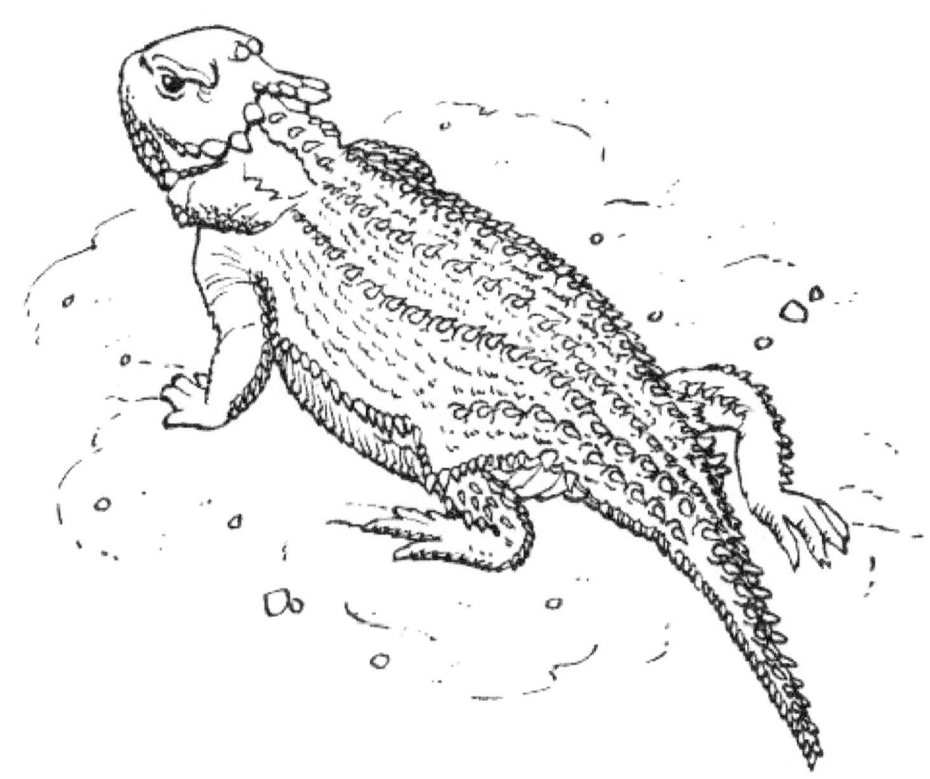

Lizard

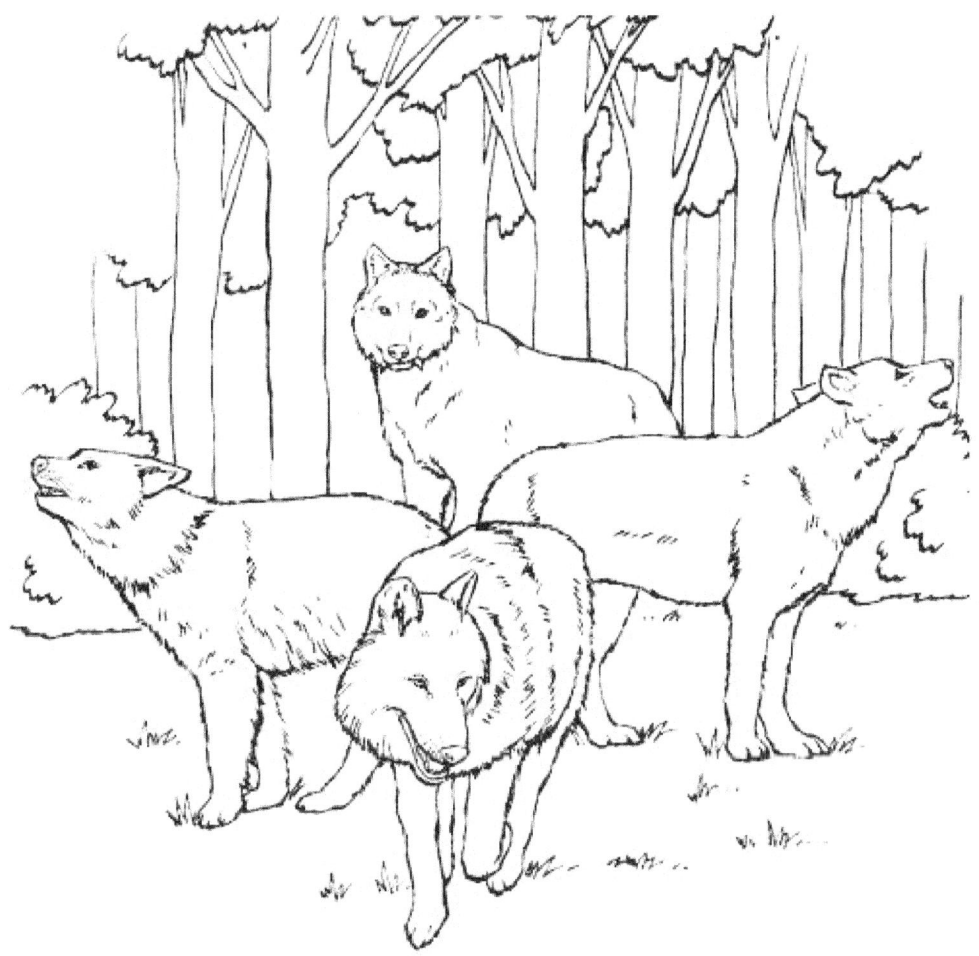

Wolves

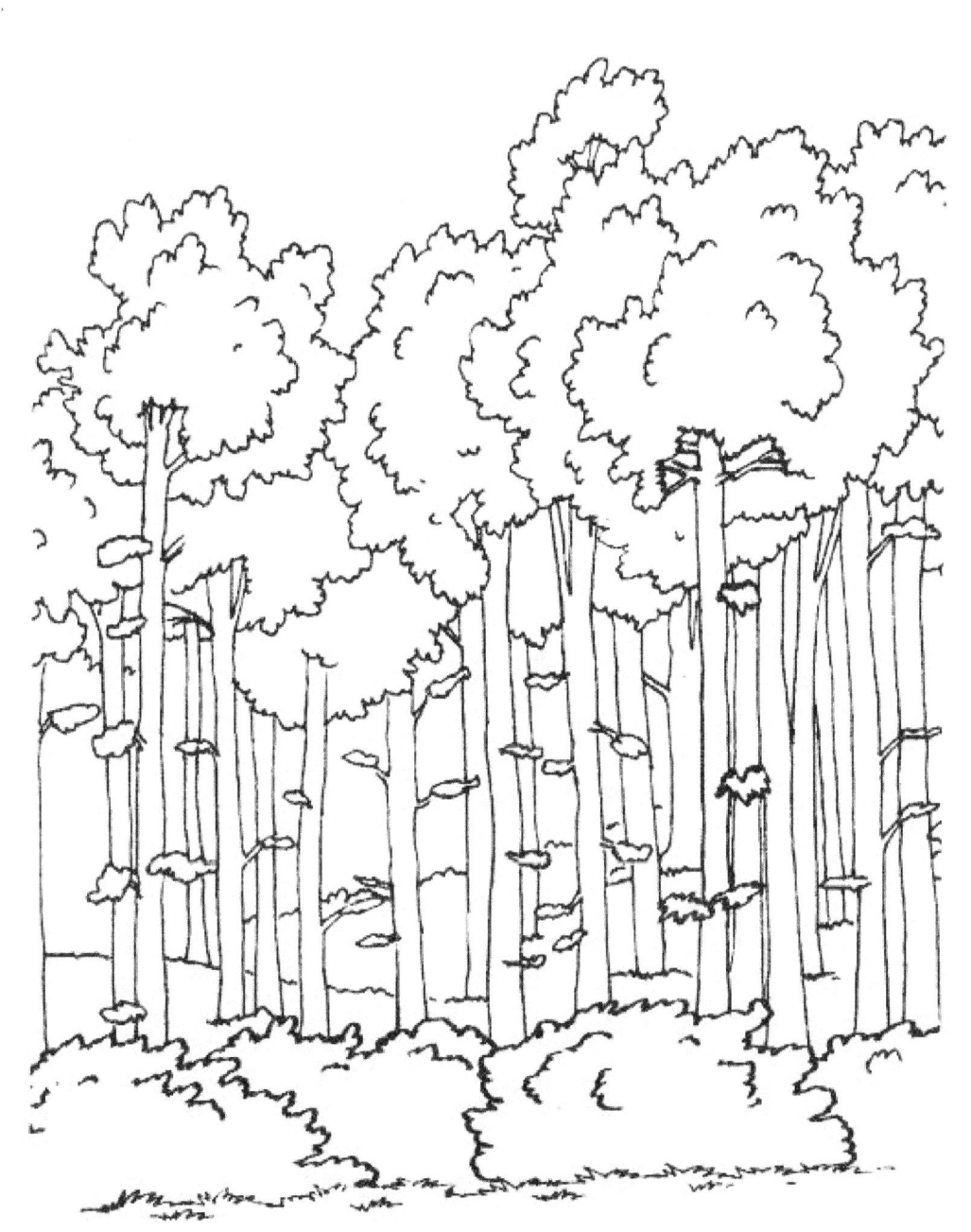

Forests cover 1/3 of the Earth's surface.

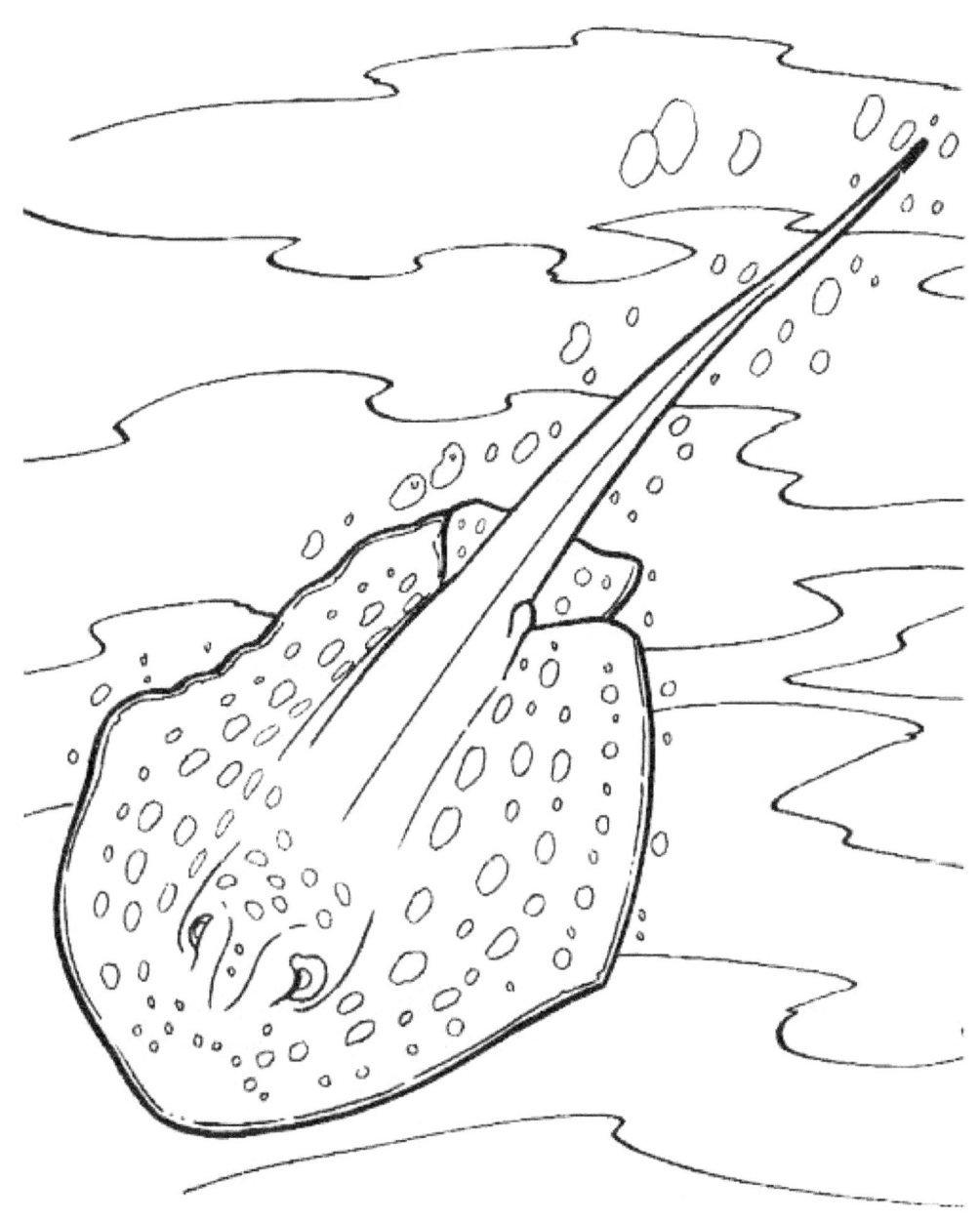

Stingray

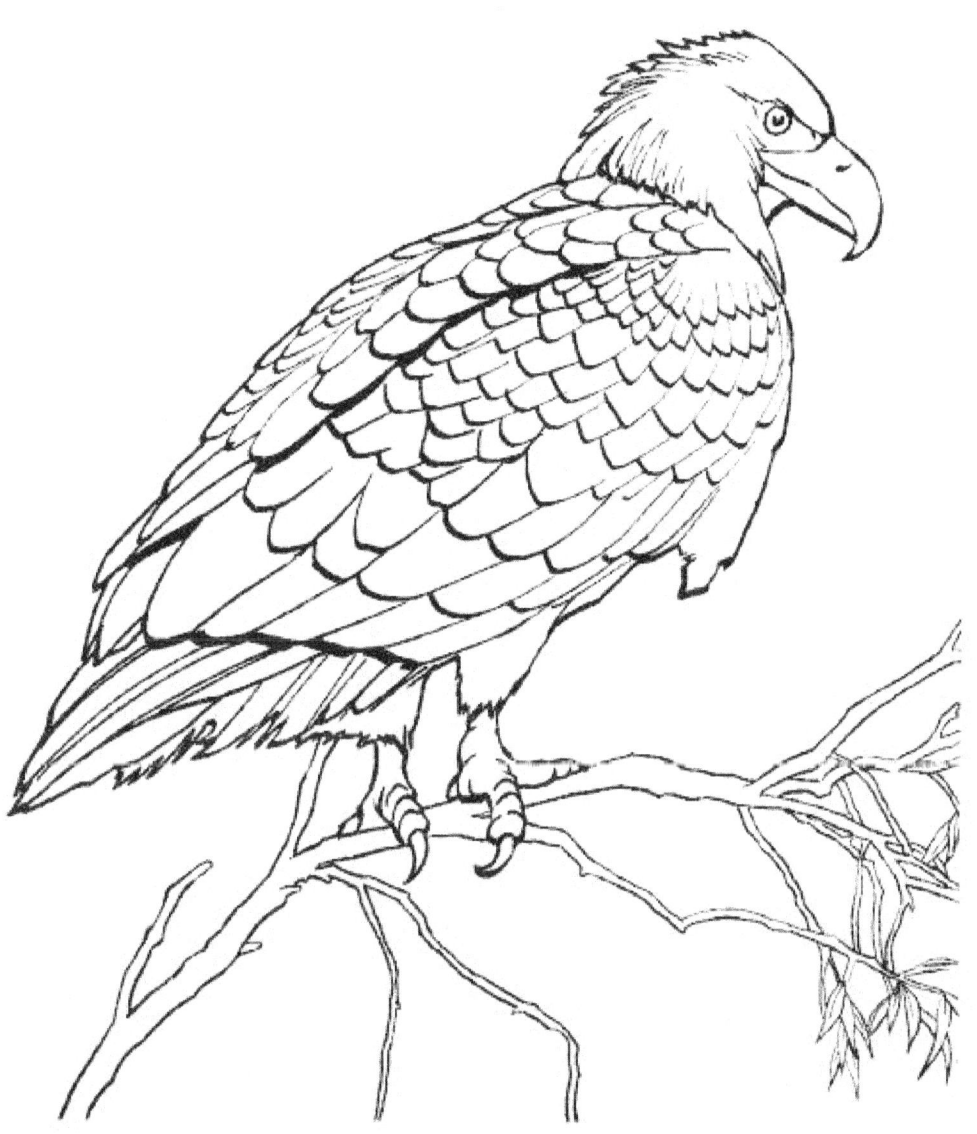

**Eagles are the most
magnificent birds of prey.**

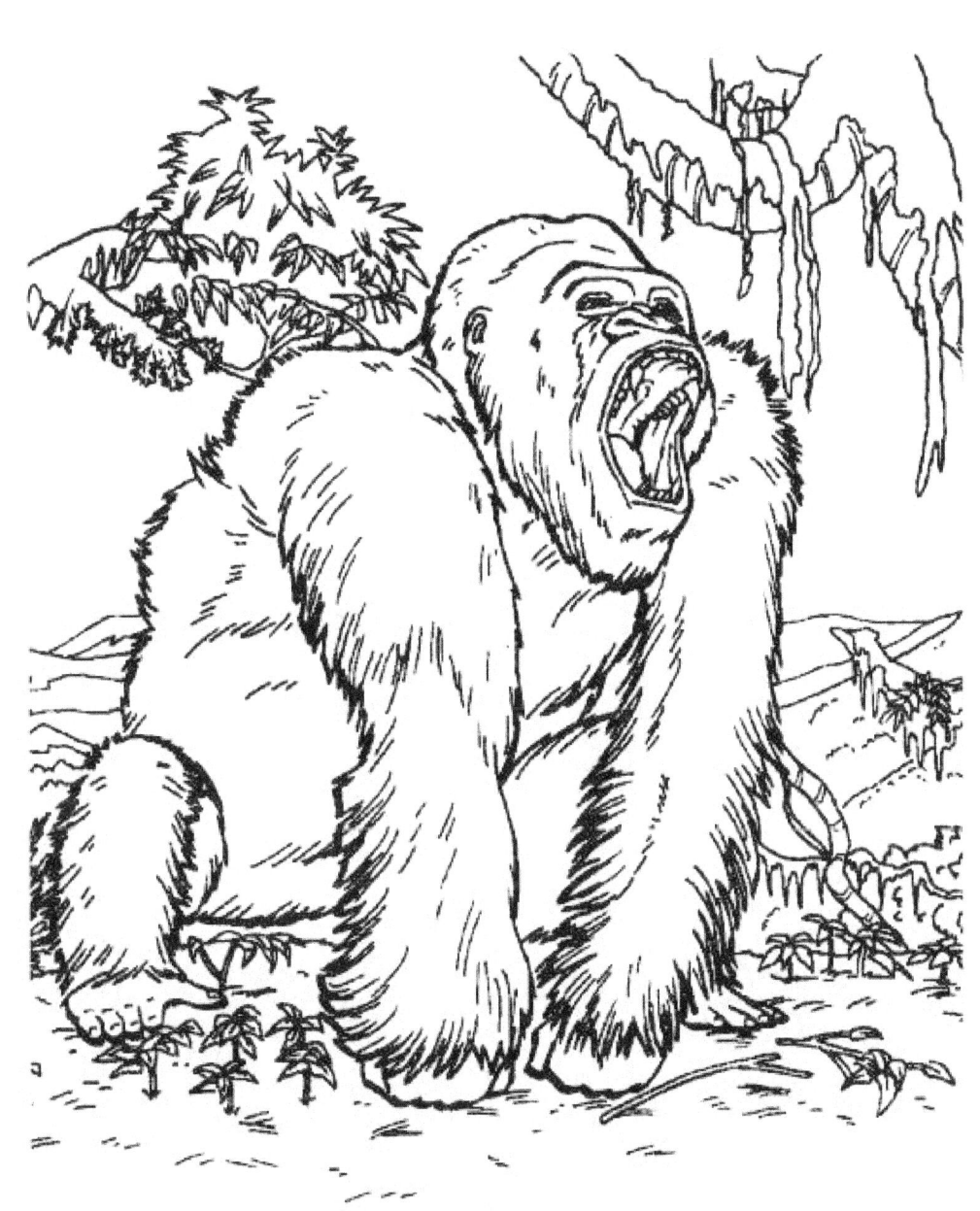

Gorilla

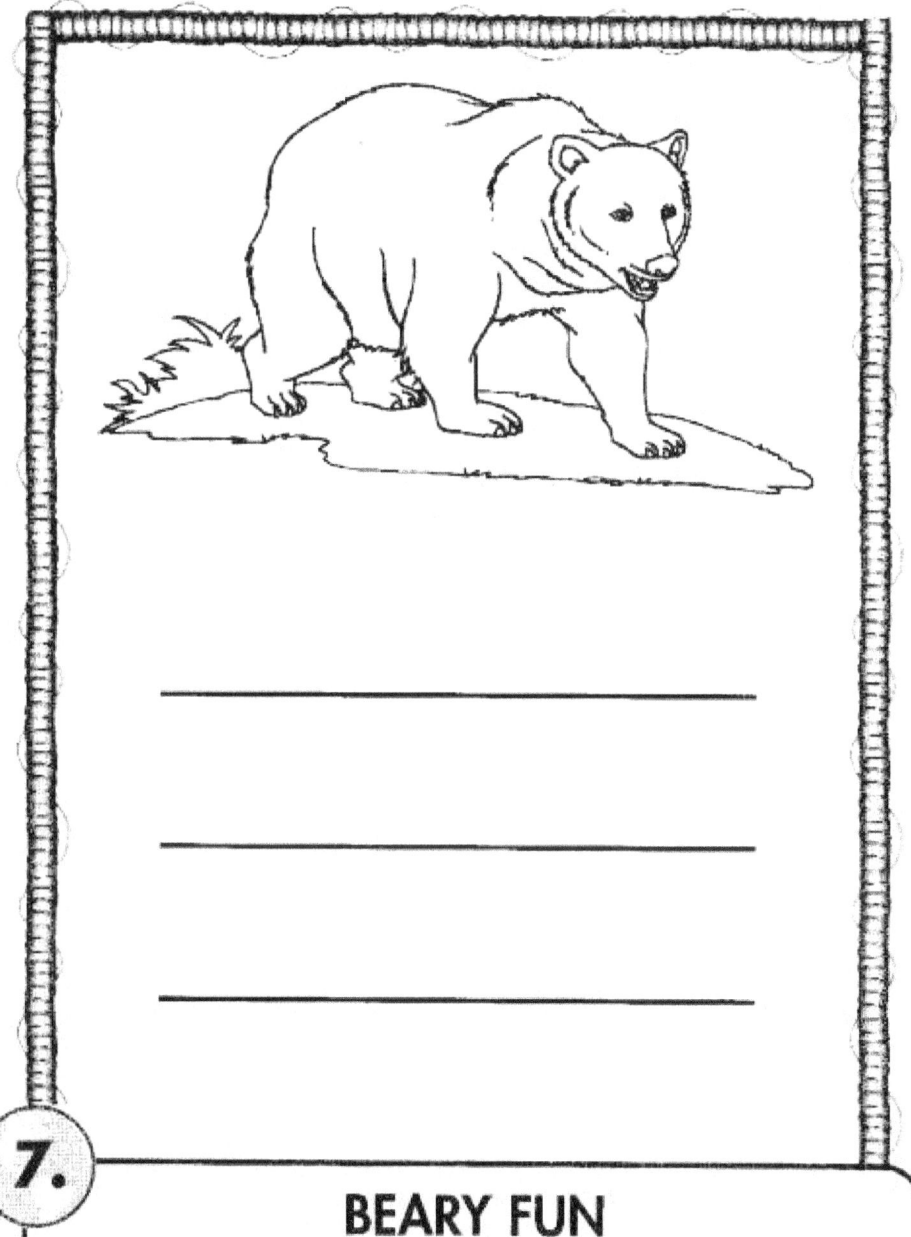

_____

_____

_____

7.

BEARY FUN

Can you name 3 different types of bears in less than 1 minute? Go!

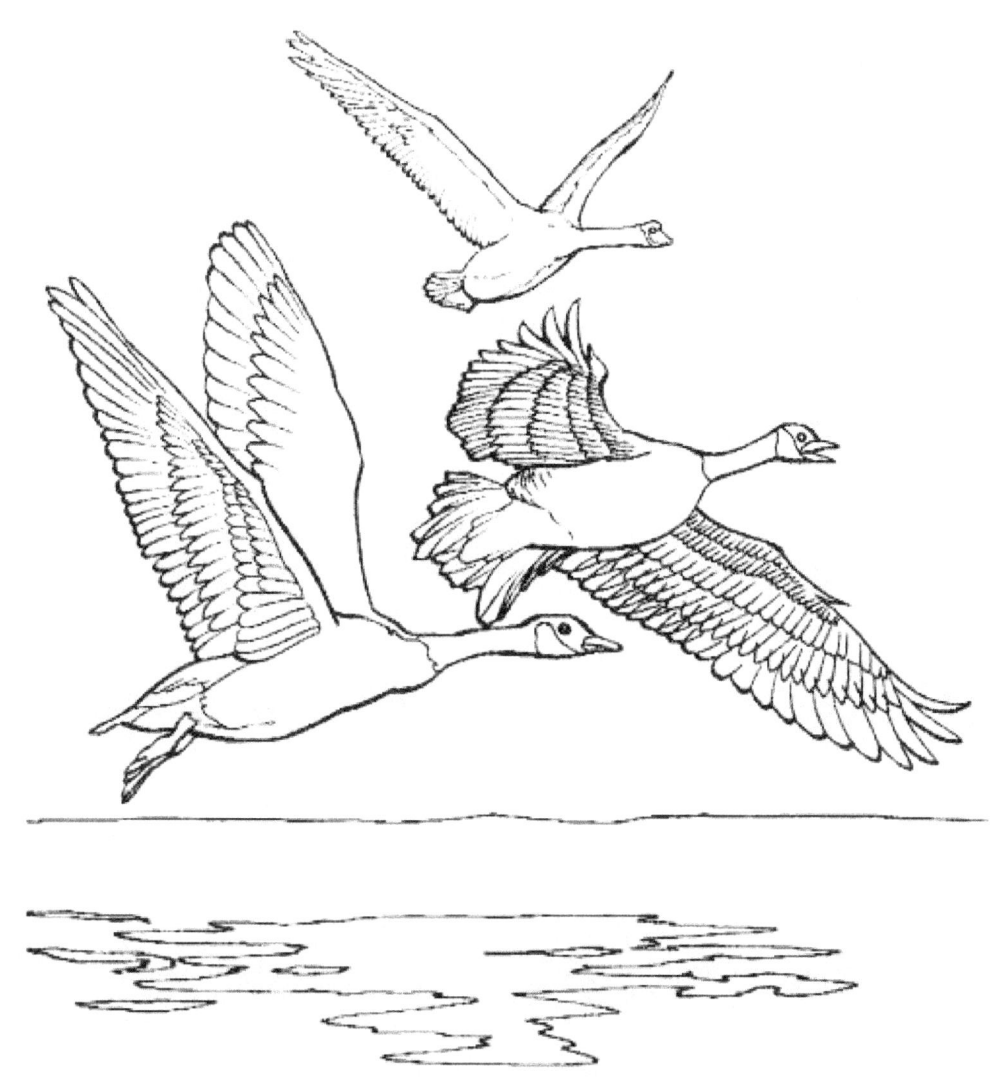

Geese

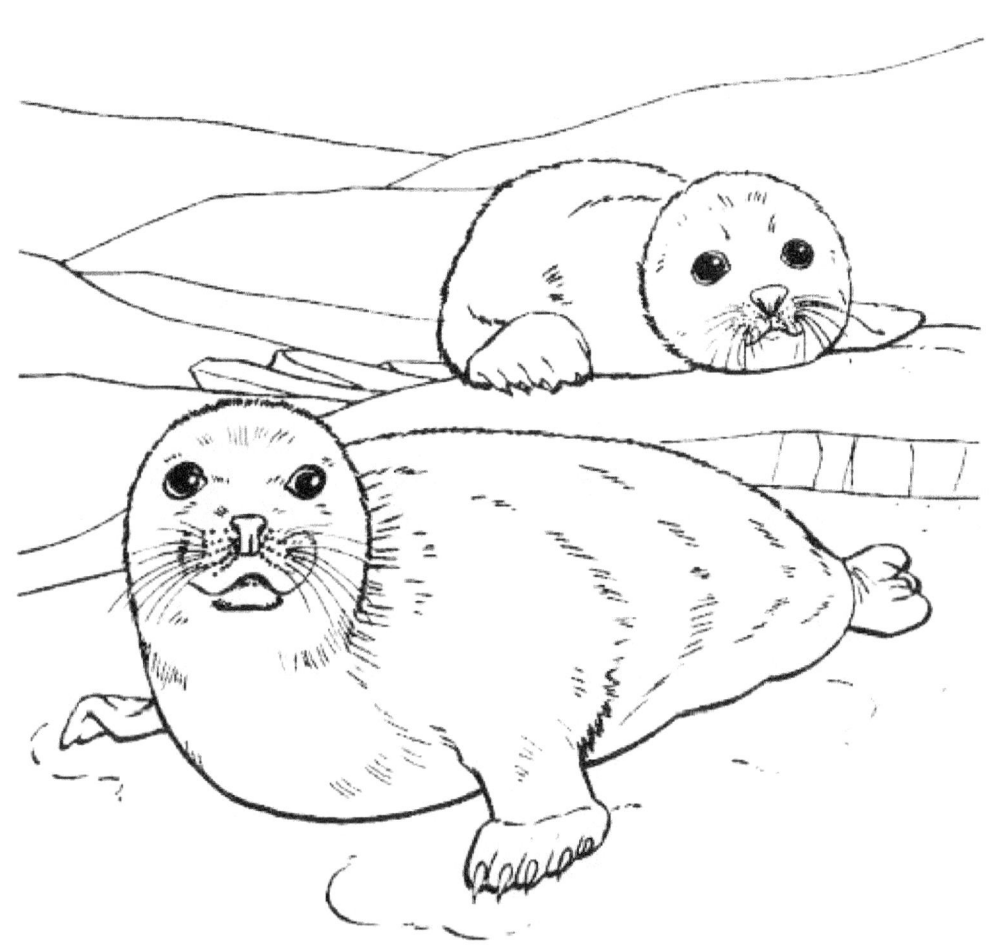

Seals

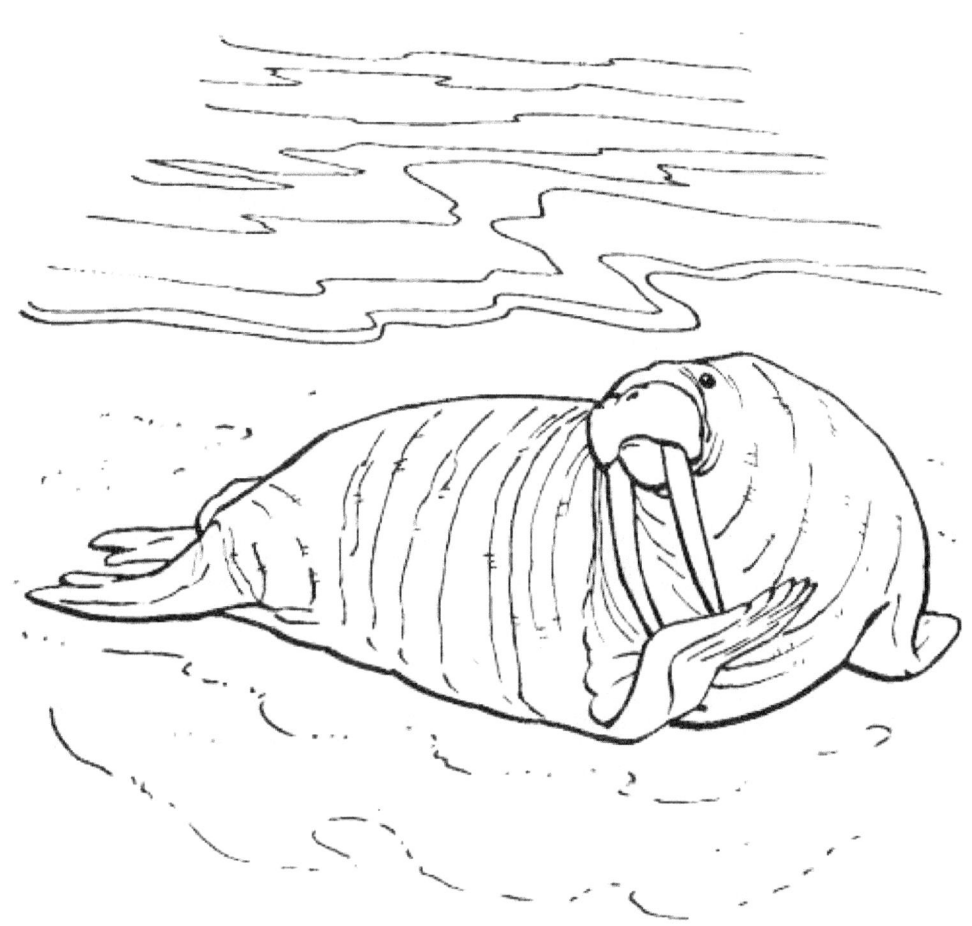

Walrus

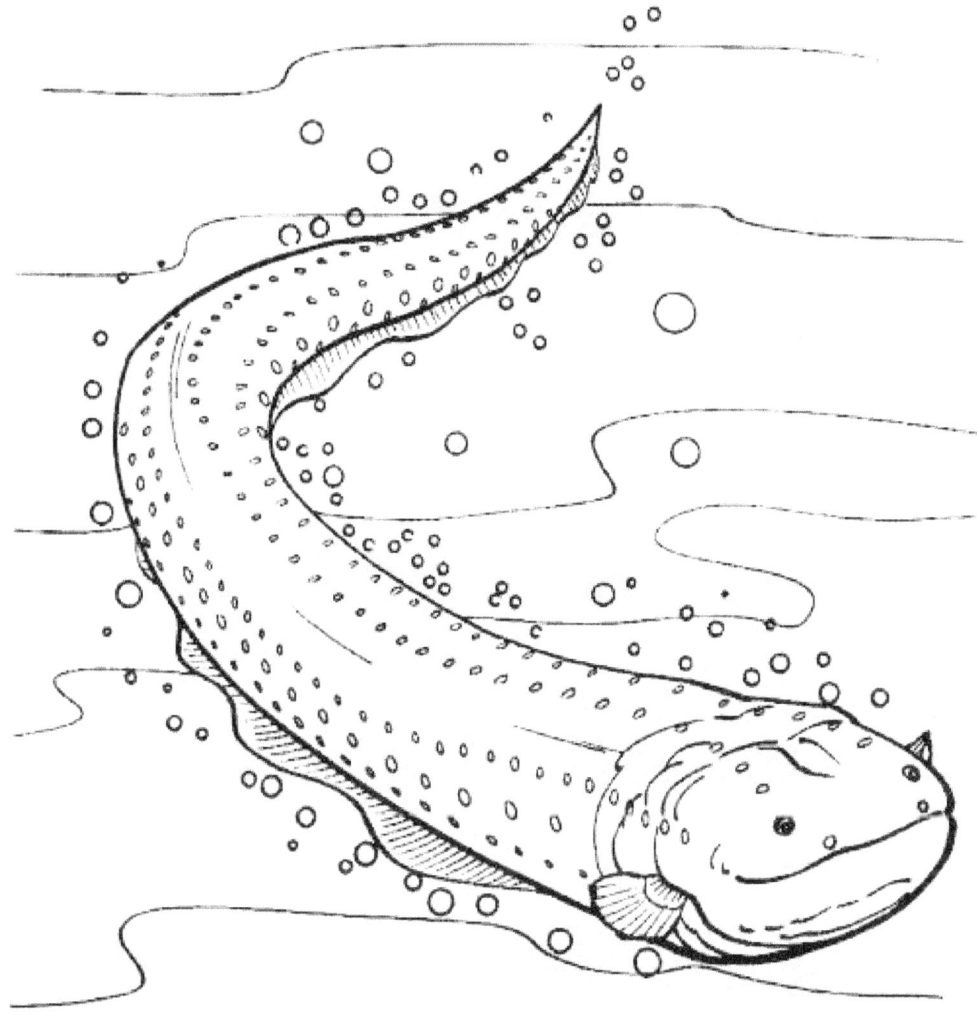

Electric Eel

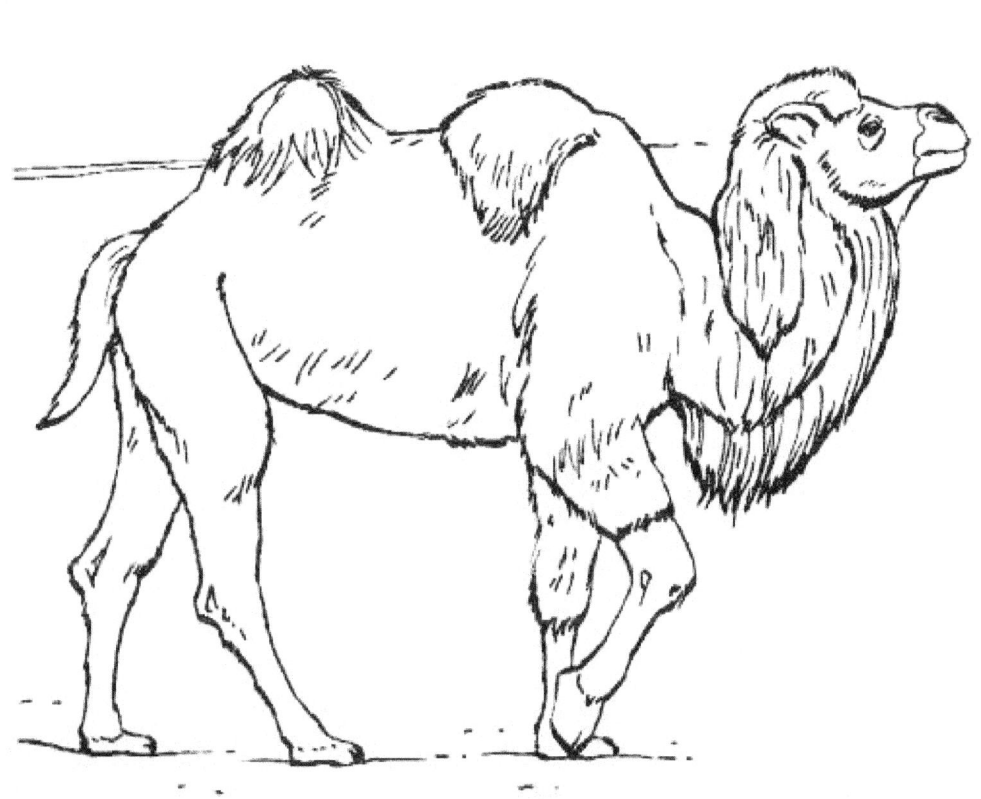

Camel

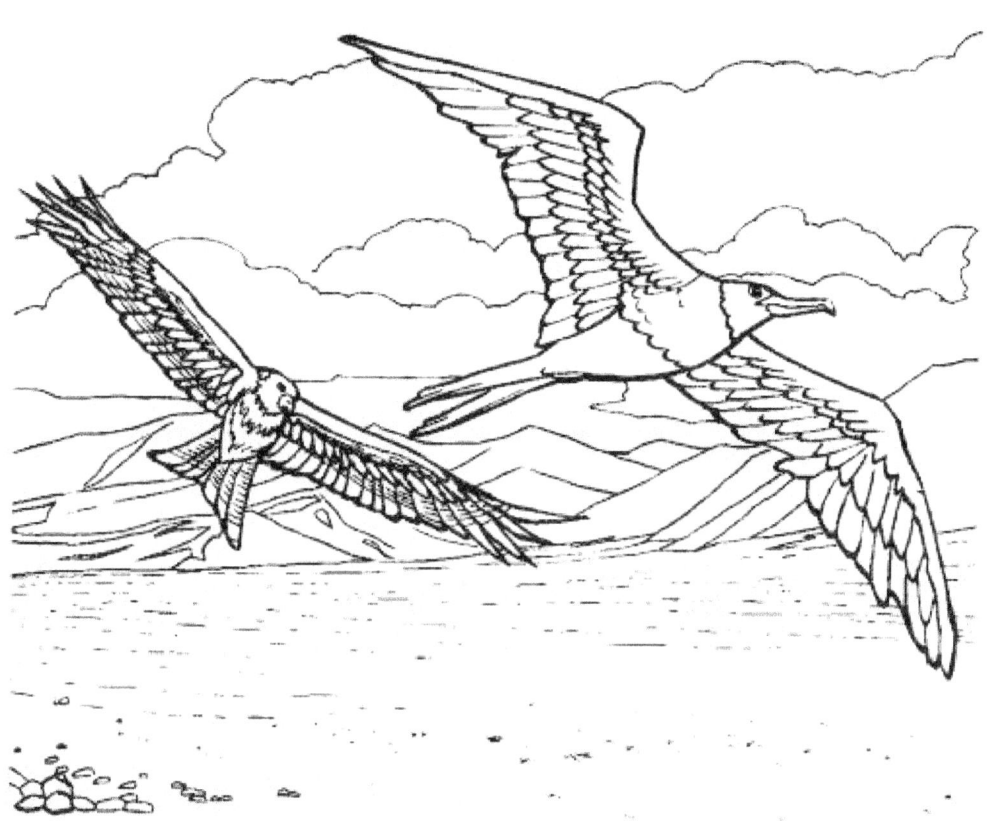

Sea Gulls

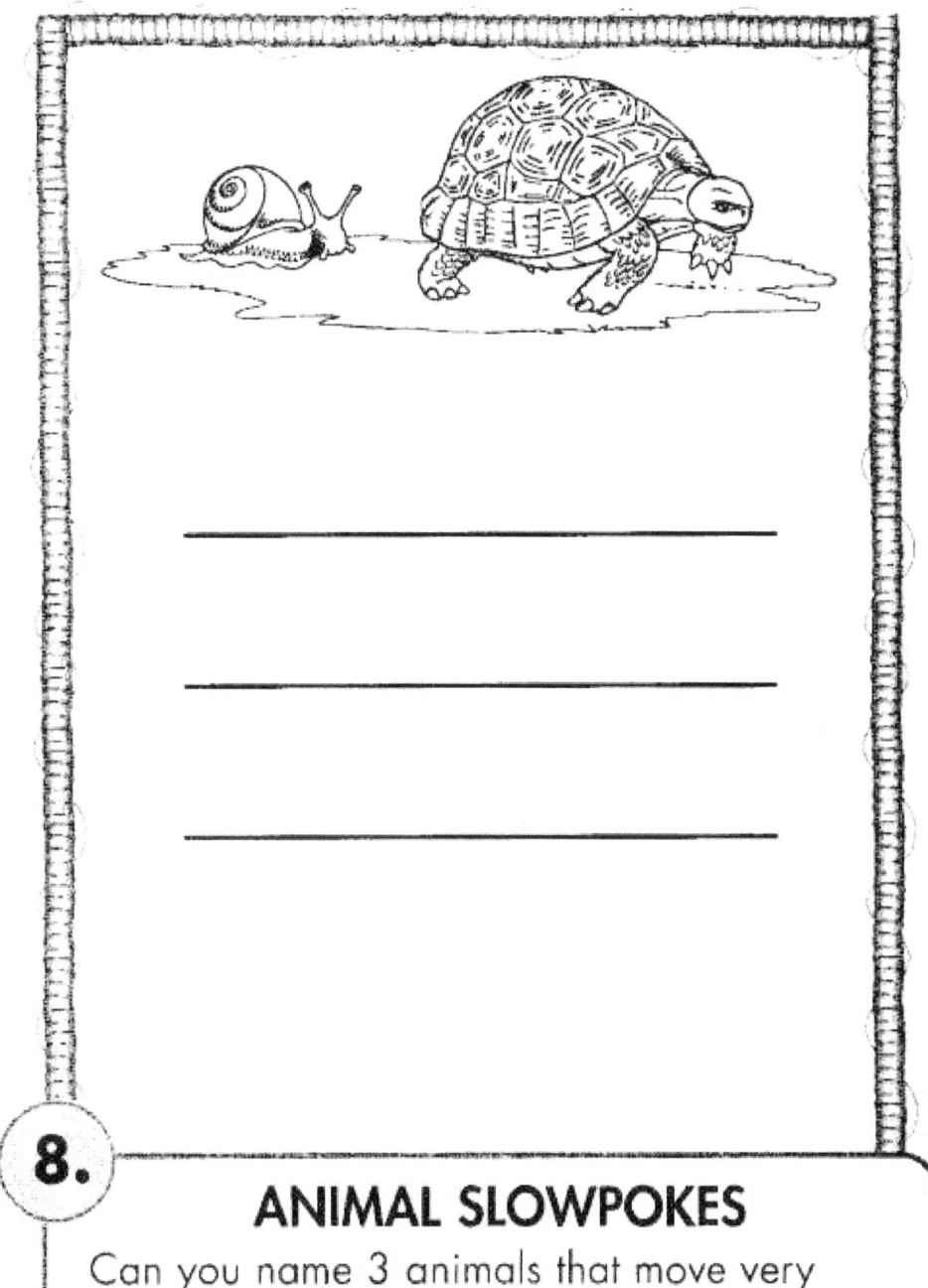

_____

_____

_____

8.

ANIMAL SLOWPOKES

Can you name 3 animals that move very slowly? Write your answers on the lines!

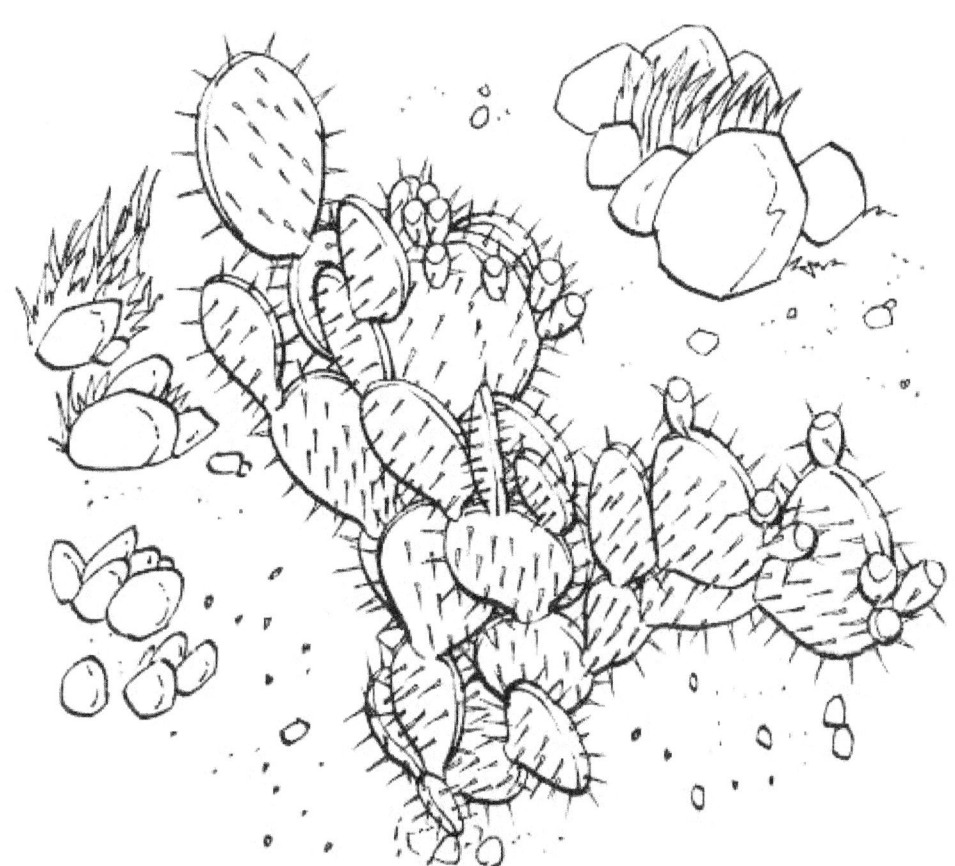

Cactus

www.ingramcontent.com/pod-product-compliance
Lightning Source LLC
Chambersburg PA
CBHW081639220526

45468CB00009B/2504